Kids Don't Come with Instruction Manuals

Basic Parenting Skills

Kristen J. Amundson

ScarecrowEducation
Lanham, Maryland • Toronto • Oxford
2004

Published in the United States of America
by ScarecrowEducation
An imprint of The Rowman & Littlefield Publishing Group, Inc.
4501 Forbes Boulevard, Suite 200, Lanham, Maryland 20706
www.scarecroweducation.com

PO Box 317
Oxford
OX2 9RU, UK

Copyright © 2004 by Kristen J. Amundson

All rights reserved. No part of this publication may be reproduced, stored in a retrieval system, or transmitted in any form or by any means, electronic, mechanical, photocopying, recording, or otherwise, without the prior permission of the publisher.

British Library Cataloguing in Publication Information Available

Library of Congress Cataloging-in-Publication Data

Amundson, Kristen J.
  Kids don't come with instruction manuals : basic parenting skills / Kristen Amundson.
     p. cm.
  Includes bibliographical references.
  ISBN 1-57886-049-0 (pbk. : alk. paper)
  1. Child rearing. 2. Parenting. I. Title.
HQ769 .A5598 2004
649'.1—dc22   2003017678

∞™ The paper used in this publication meets the minimum requirements of American National Standard for Information Sciences—Permanence of Paper for Printed Library Materials, ANSI/NISO Z39.48-1992.
Manufactured in the United States of America.

Life affords no greater responsibility, no greater privilege,
than the raising of the next generation.

— C. Everett Koop

Contents

Preface vii

1 The First Year 1
2 Toddlers 7
3 The Preschool Years 13
4 The Elementary School Years 19
5 Early Adolescence 25
6 The High School Years 29

References 37

About the Author 40

Preface

Babies don't come with instruction manuals. There's no recipe book to tell you how to teach a child the important lessons of life—how to be responsible, how to tell the truth, how to develop self-discipline and self-confidence. Yet these are the most basic of basic skills—the things that will make children successful in school *and* in life.

As a parent, you may not always feel you've had much preparation for such an important responsibility. You may have had few opportunities to care for younger brothers and sisters when you were growing up. And you may currently live too far away from your own parents to rely on them for advice.

Even when you think you've figured things out, your child will change again. The techniques that worked yesterday suddenly don't work today. You may find yourself wishing for a little "on-the-job training."

You know that parents are vital to children's development. How can you do the best job in this important task? In his reassuring book on child-rearing, *A Good Enough Parent*, noted child psychologist Bruno Bettleheim suggests that it is not necessary to be a "perfect parent":

> *In order to raise a child well one ought not to try to be a perfect parent, as much as one should not expect one's child to be, or to become, a perfect individual. Perfection is not within the grasp of ordinary human beings. But it is quite possible to be a good enough parent—that is, a parent who raises his child well. (p. xi)*

This publication, like its predecessor, *Parenting Skills: Bringing Out the Best in Your Child* (1989), is designed to be a resource for parents who want to understand more about how children grow and develop . . . and what they, the parents, can do to help them along their way. It includes information on how children develop the independence, self-discipline, self-confidence, and skills in communication and cooperation with others that will help them throughout their lives. It also includes suggested resources that can provide additional advice and answers to your questions. Most importantly, it will help you bring out the best in your child.

1
The First Year

"The greatness of the human personality," observed educator Maria Montessori, "begins at the hour of birth." Doctors can predict many things about a newborn's personality soon after a child is born. Learning to accept and respond to your child's unique character traits is one of the biggest challenges of the first year of life.

Researchers now know that babies are born with certain traits, often referred to as the child's "temperament." From the landmark study by the husband-and-wife team of psychologists Alexander Thomas and Stella Chess, who began doing long-term research on temperament in the 1950s, it is clear that babies are different from one another right from the start.

Some babies gurgle and coo when they see new faces. Others are much slower to warm up to a new person or a new food. Some babies laugh and smile. Others don't show much emotion.

If you have a baby who is excessively fussy, it may not be the result of anything you are doing wrong. In fact, most babies seem to have a fussy period at the end of the day. Some parents worry that by picking up a fussy baby, they may run the risk of "spoiling" him. *Note:* Because this book is about a very important individual—your child—we have used the singular pronoun throughout. We have, however, tried to alternate "he" and "she." All advice in this booklet is designed for both boys and girls.

You will be relieved to know that your basic instinct—to pick up your baby and comfort him—is important in helping him develop. As Marguerite Kelly and Elia Parsons (1992) explain it:

> *The cries of a helpless baby must be answered, even if neither of you knows what's the matter. If a child learns she can depend on you in her first year she'll obey you in later ones, for she listens best to people who listen to her.* (p. 81)

During the first year, when your child is growing and learning more than she ever will again in her life, your challenge is to help her learn to cope with all those changes in a way that's right for her. As you learn more about the special qualities of your baby, both of you will be setting the stage for a lifetime relationship unlike any other. No matter how many children you have, each will be different and raising each will be special.

Childcare

Childcare is a fact of life for many families. In 2001, three of every five preschoolers had a mother in the workforce (Children's Defense Fund, 2001). So for most families today, the decision is not whether a mother will return to work after a baby is born, but *when*.

In some cases, the family has little choice and the mother must return to her job as soon as possible. But most experts say that, if possible, the mother (or father) should plan to spend at least the first four months at home. Leaving before that, says Brazelton (1992), is "awfully hard on [the parent]." The first three months of life are turbulent. "Four months gives [the parent] time to get through the fussy three-month period and enjoy a month of pleasure, with the baby smiling and gurgling at her" (p. 80).

Of course, when the time comes, it's important to choose a caregiver carefully. There are many alternatives. Often a relative may care for the child. You may bring someone into your home. You may take your child to a daycare provider who cares for several children in her home. Or you may enroll your child in a more traditional childcare center.

Which of these is best? Like everything else about raising children, the answer is, "It depends." Some approaches work better with some children than others. Your responsibility is to choose the care that works best for your child and your family. Then stay in close touch to make sure your child continues to receive the attention needed to grow and develop.

Questions to Ask as You Choose Childcare

- Does your child have any special needs? Will the daycare provider be able to meet your child's needs?
- What kind of childcare fits your budget? For low-income families, programs such as federally funded Head Start are available. Many states also fund childcare. Either call your local library for the phone numbers for these programs or search for local childcare programs on the Internet. Many families may be entitled to childcare credits on their state and federal income tax.
- How clean and attractive is the daycare site?
- How safe are the children while in childcare? Are they supervised wherever they go? (About half of all injuries children suffer in childcare come when they are playing outside.)
- Do the childcare provider's hours match your schedule? (You will not want to feel stressed every day if you leave work even one or two minutes late.)
- How does the childcare provider handle meal times? Would you be able to send in special food for your child?

> - At naptime, can your child have her own special blankets, pillows, or stuffed toys?
> - Do the caregivers seem to enjoy the children? Do the children look relaxed and involved with what is going on?
> - Are there lots of things for children to do? Are there plenty of books?
> - As a parent, do you feel comfortable? Could you imagine your child at this site? (Mays and Cohen, 2002)

Safety

Accidents pose the greatest single health threat to children and are the leading cause of death of children under the age of four (American Academy of Pediatrics, 2003). But most injuries can be prevented. Here are ways of protecting your child from two of the leading causes of infant deaths:

Automobile injuries. Fasten children correctly into a child safety seat *every time* they ride in your car. The safest place for children is in the back seat of the car, with or without air bags. Once children reach the age of four and weigh forty pounds, use a booster or harness system until they are big enough to use a regular seat belt. *Never, ever leave your child alone in the car.*

Suffocation. The slats on the side of a crib or playpen should be no more than 2 3/8 inches apart. Keep plastic bags and balloons away from small children. Because small children can choke on small objects, keep buttons, small parts of objects, and small toys away from babies or toddlers. Round or hard foods like hot dogs, nuts, hard candies, raw carrots, or popcorn are dangerous for children under four. Learn the Heimlich maneuver, infant and child CPR, and first aid.

Learning Language

From the day your child is born (and, according to some research, even before that), she is learning language. Language is the foundation of all other learning, and your child acquires it at home. You can help by talking with her as much as possible. When you're dressing her, for example, you can say things like, "Now we'll put the shoe on your foot."

Speaking requires children to develop control over a great many small muscles, so most children will not say more than a few words during their first year of life. But you'll recognize that even at an early age, your child *understands* a great many more words than she is able to *speak*.

2
Toddlers

"Children need models more than they need critics," wrote Frenchman Joseph Joubert in 1842. That advice is never more true . . . or more difficult to follow . . . than when your child is a toddler. The toddler years, generally ages 1 to 3, are a time when your child develops independence, which he will do mostly by testing every rule and boundary that he encounters.

It's no coincidence that so many parents speak about "the terrible twos" since children at this age can be difficult. But in all his struggles with you, your child is working on his primary task: forging a sense of himself as an individual. He needs your support and love to recognize that his need for autonomy is accepted—even if the specific methods he chooses to exercise his independence are not.

Discipline

This is the age when discipline becomes an issue in many families because this is the time when children need parents to set limits. By establishing guidelines for appropriate behavior now, you will be setting the stage for the *self-discipline* your child will need to become successful in school and later in life.

The word *discipline* really means *teaching*, or "training that develops self-control." Discipline doesn't come from anger. It doesn't involve embarrassing a child. It doesn't destroy a child's sense of worth. The goal of discipline is to help your child develop the ability to guide her own behavior, even when you aren't there.

Most experts say that your family discipline policies should be based on two important guidelines:

Ensuring your child's safety. One pediatrician explained, "When your child is reaching for a hot pan on the stove, that is *not* the time to discuss possible consequences. It's a time to grab the child's hand and say a firm 'NO.'"

Helping establish a routine and structure for your child's life. You'll have fewer pitched battles about clothing if it's simply the rule that everyone must be dressed before breakfast—and if you don't worry too much when your child wears the orange striped shirt with the red checked pants.

Allow for Choices

A toddler's favorite word is "No," so many parents don't ask questions that can be answered with that word. Instead of asking, "Do you want lunch?" give your child a choice. "Would you like peanut butter or cheese on your sandwich?" "Do you want yogurt or cheese?"

Giving choices will avoid power struggles. But it is also a good way to help build your child's sense of independence and self-esteem.

Saying "No" and Meaning It

Here's a scene we've all seen in the grocery store: A toddler is screaming for a candy bar. He cries and carries on. Finally, his mother buys the candy just to stop the crying. That toddler just learned the wrong lesson. It might take ten minutes of acting out, but eventually Mom and Dad will give in.

One of the hardest lessons parents need to learn about discipline is that they have to be consistent. If you say "no," then you have to follow through.

Focus on the Positive

Discipline is easier if you emphasize the positive rather than the negative. So you say, "Let's hurry to bed so we can read your favorite book," instead of "I want you in bed *this minute*." You'll find this positive technique works on children (and adults) of all ages.

Time Out

When your child has broken a rule, try giving a "time out." Put him in a quiet place for one minute per year of age. (Try a spare bedroom or a quiet corner rather than your child's room. There, he'll probably just play with his toys.) Give a short, calm talk about why he's going into time out. "We do not call other people names." Then walk away.

What about spanking? A 1997 study found that spanking actually tends to *create* more bad behavior than it corrects (Strauss, Sugarman, and Giles-Simms, 1997).

> "Adults teach children in three important ways:
> The first is by example, the second is by example, the third is by example."
> — Albert Schweitzer

Temper Tantrums

Finally, a word about temper tantrums. (Yes, your child will have them, and probably in a public place.) As difficult as tantrums are for an adult to deal with, they are normal. For most children, tantrums peak during the second year, which is why this year is so often called "the terrible twos."

Tantrums aren't your fault. Most toddlers don't have the language skills they need to express their feelings. For them, a tantrum is simply a way of letting you know that they are unhappy or frustrated. That will be small comfort when your child is lying in the middle of the grocery store aisle kicking his feet, but it will help you to know that children who *don't* have tantrums now are more likely to become hot-tempered teens or adults (Brazelton, p.155).

Reading Aloud

If you haven't done so already, you'll want to begin the habit of reading to your child every day. Study after study shows that the single most important way parents can help their children become good readers is to read aloud every day.

Your reading time is a special time you share with your child. Here are some tips on reading aloud with toddlers:

Make reading part of your routine. Pick a quiet time, such as just before bed. Many children love to read snuggled in their parents' lap, and it's a comforting routine for parents as well. If your child gets tired or restless, stop reading. It should be fun for both you and your child.

Try to read to your child every day. If you're just starting out, read for a few minutes, several times a day. Later, you can stretch the time. If you have to skip a day or two, just get back to your routine as soon as you can.

As you read, talk with your child. Ask questions. "Look at that red bird. That's a cardinal. Do you remember when we saw a cardinal in the park?"

Reread favorite books. Children often have a book that they want parents to read again and again (and again and again). You may become tired of the same book. But your child will continue to learn from hearing it read again and again.

Read "predictable" books. These are books with a word or an action that appears over and over. These books help children learn to predict what will happen next. That's a skill they need for the rest of their reading life!

Visit the library. Start when your child is very young. When your child can get his first library card, make it a day to celebrate. Be sure you check out some books, too; seeing parents read is one way to encourage children to read.

If you're uncomfortable with your reading ability, find out about adult reading programs. Ask the librarian or check the Internet for some programs in your community (U.S. Department of Education, 2000).

3
The Preschool Years

Once children have realized that they're separate individuals, they move on to the next crucial stage in their development—developing competence. During the preschool years, typically ages 3 to 5, your child will be striving to master herself and her environment.

Because the list of things children are *not* able to do is still longer than the things they *are* able to do, they need your help so they can do as much as possible for themselves. This means:

- Clothes that are easy to put on and take off.
- Step stools that allow a child to reach faucets. (But be careful of step stools in the kitchen, where children may also reach hot burners.)
- Sturdy toys and books that will stand up to some rough treatment.
- Low shelves and coat hooks that make it easier to put possessions where they belong.
- At least a few pieces of furniture scaled to your child's size.

Learning to Communicate

"Children who are not spoken to by live and responsive adults will not learn to speak properly. Children who are not answered will stop asking questions. They will become incurious. And children who are not told stories and who are not read to will have few reasons for wanting to learn to read."
— Gayle E. Haley, Caldecott Medal acceptance speech

Your interaction with your child is key to developing his language skills. In your day-to-day conversations with your child, speak in complete sentences—and encourage him to do the same. Teach your child nursery rhymes and say them aloud together. Singing also helps language development. Young children enjoy almost any kind of music—children's songs, rock music, folk tunes, hymns, or whatever kind of music you enjoy.

Helping your child develop strong listening and speaking skills will also build a foundation for success in reading later on. Here are some pointers to playing with your child to help increase her vocabulary and her ability to use and understand language:

- Play a "first sound" game. Start with sounds that are easy to hear—the "s" sound or the first sound in your child's name. See how many things you can find that start with that sound.
- Rhyming is a skill children need as they learn to sound out words. When words rhyme, their ending sounds stay the same, but their beginning sounds change. Look for books that include many rhyming words. Learn nursery rhymes.
- Help your child make letters out of modeling clay.
- Buy an inexpensive set of magnetic letters for your refrigerator. Together with your child, find the letters with curves. Find the

letters with straight lines. Sort the letters in as many different ways as you and your child can think of. As you are sorting, talk about the features of the letters and what makes them the same or different (U.S. Department of Education, 1993).

Building Responsibility

The preschool years are *not* too early for children to take some responsibility for caring for themselves and their surroundings. Responsibility builds self-confidence and self-esteem, and it's vital to success in school and on the job.

So your preschoolers can and should be expected to pick up toys (though not by themselves and not without gentle prompting); dress themselves (as long as you don't worry if shirts are worn back-to-front at least some of the time); and help with some of the chores of family life, such as setting the table and dusting.

Children learn habits of responsibility if you:

- Expect them,
- Model them, and
- Participate in them.

In other words, you don't tell a preschooler, "Clean your room." Instead, you say, "I'll put the books on the shelf. You find all the toys with wheels and put them in the basket."

Play

Play is the primary way children develop during the preschool years. Through play, children:

- Develop their large muscles through vigorous exercise such as running, jumping, climbing, and riding tricycles.
- Learn fine muscle coordination through such activities as coloring, cutting, pasting, and working with puzzles.
- Learn how to occupy themselves when they are alone.
- Learn to cooperate with others when in a group.
- Develop their imaginations.
- Learn language.

Parents can help their children develop through play by providing a variety of different experiences—some indoors and some outdoors; some noisy and some quiet; some initiated by parents and others following the child's lead.

You don't have to spend a lot of money on toys. Low-cost toys such as crayons and clay provide a lot of play value. Many toys children love don't cost any money at all—just some creativity. A cardboard tube from a roll of paper towels can become a rocket, a telescope, or a castle tower. An old bath towel can become a superhero's cape or a fairy princess's gown.

Choosing a Preschool

For years, research has shown that the effects of a good early educational experience last through life. The famous study of the Perry Preschool Project found that those children who attended preschool:

- Were better prepared intellectually and socially for school.
- Progressed better through school, with higher achievement and a greater likelihood to complete homework.
- Were more likely to graduate from high school.
- Were more likely to attend some type of postsecondary education.

But what is a "quality" preschool? The National Association for the Education of Young Children (NAEYC) suggests you look for these ten signs to make sure your child is in a good classroom:

1. Children spend most of their time playing and working with materials or other children. They do not wander aimlessly and they are not expected to sit quietly for long periods of time.
2. Children have access to various activities throughout the day. Look for assorted building blocks and other construction materials, props for pretend play, picture books, paints and other art materials, and table toys such as matching games, pegboards, and puzzles. Children should not all be doing the same thing at the same time.
3. Teachers work with individual children, small groups, and the whole group at different times during the day. They do not spend all their time with the whole group.

4. The classroom is decorated with children's original artwork, their own writing with invented spelling, and stories dictated by children to teachers.
5. Children learn numbers and the alphabet in the context of their everyday experiences. The natural world of plants and animals and meaningful activities like cooking, taking attendance, or serving snack provide the basis for learning activities.
6. Children work on projects and have long periods of time (at least one hour) to play and explore. Worksheets are used little if at all.
7. Children have an opportunity to play outside every day, weather permitting. Outdoor play is never sacrificed for more instructional time.
8. Teachers read books to children individually or in small groups throughout the day, not just at group story time.
9. The curriculum is adapted for those who are ahead as well as those who need additional help. Teachers recognize that children's different backgrounds and experiences mean that they do not learn the same things at the same time in the same way.
10. Children and their parents look forward to school. Parents feel secure about sending their child to the program. Children are happy to attend; they do not cry regularly or complain of feeling sick.

4
The Elementary School Years

When your child enters elementary school, he begins to identify more closely with friends and teachers. Acceptance from peers is vital for children between ages 6 and 12. Friends provide mirrors in which your child learns to see himself.

It's about this time that your child experiences a dramatic change in the way he thinks about the world. He begins to realize that he is not the center of the universe, and that the world outside himself is not magic, but governed by certain discoverable laws. In the model of child development first proposed by Jean Piaget, the child has moved from the "preoperational" stage to the stage of "concrete operations." In other words, children at this age want to learn how things work.

Parents are very important in this new age of discovery. In fact, your acceptance and love will provide your child with a continuous opportunity to "recharge his batteries" as he moves toward learning to stand on his own. These are the years to help your child develop academic, physical, and social skills.

Success in School

"When parents are involved in their children's education at home, they do better in school. And when parents are involved in school, children go farther in school—and the schools they go to are better" (Henderson and Berla, 1994).

Researchers have examined hundreds of studies on parental involvement. Those studies show these positive benefits for students whose parents are involved, including:

- Higher grades and test scores
- Improved reading scores
- Regular school attendance
- Positive attitude and appropriate behavior

Parent Involvement in School

As a parent, your involvement with the school is key to your child's performance. Here are just some of the ways you can increase your involvement in and impact on your child's education. (Contact your child's teacher or principal to find other ways you can help.)

- Become a member of your school's parent-teacher organization or join the school's Title I parents' group, a bilingual advisory committee or a parent group sponsored by ASPIRA, NAACP, or the Urban League. The earlier that parental involvement begins

in a child's educational process, the more powerful the effects (Cotton and Wikelund, 2001).
- Visit a class to talk about your career.
- Invite a class to visit your workplace. Set up a "volunteer bank" noting parents' special interests and abilities.
- Attend a school-sponsored play, performance, or athletic event.
- Attend a school board meeting.
- Serve on a building or district-based committee, advisory group, or task force.
- See how you can help with a project in or out of the classroom. Lend a hand in the library. Set up a computer. Build a bookshelf for a classroom. Make phone calls to other parents. Bake cookies for a school event. Sign up to chaperon a school field trip. All these are ways to show teachers that you want to help them in their important work.

Testing

Students have always taken tests in school, but today there's a new emphasis on standardized tests. Many states already require students to pass tests in subjects such as math and reading. By the 2005/2006 school year, the federal government will also require this testing for students in public or charter schools.

Some parents support the new focus on testing. They believe that the tests have helped raise standards for all children. Other parents worry that too much time is being spent on testing. They're afraid that other important lessons may be lost while teachers focus on test-taking skills. Like them or hate them, however, the tests are probably here to stay. As a parent, there are a number of ways you can help your child prepare for standardized tests.

Get informed. Find out which tests your child will take. Write the dates for the testing on your family calendar. Make sure your child is in school on those days—don't schedule a visit to the doctor or the dentist.

Ask questions. The National Education Association suggests that parents ask these questions about the tests their child will be taking:

- How does the material my child learns in class relate to what is covered on the state tests?
- In what other ways does the school—and my child's teacher—measure how well my child is learning?
- Does my child's performance on state-required achievement tests match her performance in the classroom? (If an achievement test is not well matched to what your child is being taught at school, she could score poorly on the achievement test while still making good grades.)
- How will the school—and my child's teacher—use test results? (National Education Association, 2002)

Help at home. Ask your child's teacher what you can do at home to help your child prepare. You might review math facts, for example.

Focus on reading. If your child struggles with reading, or if he isn't interested in reading, talk about what you can do at home.

Promote a positive attitude. Some children get very nervous before taking a big test. Let your child know that you know he can do well on the test. Make sure he gets a good night's sleep and eats a healthy breakfast before taking a test. Since children don't do as well on tests if they are too hot or too cold, send a sweater that your child can take off if he gets too warm.

Encourage your child to check answers carefully. Careless errors can cost your child several points.

A New Kind of Literacy

Today, it's not enough for students to know how to read books. They also need to know how to use new technology. But parents sometimes worry about whether their child will be safe online. Here are some ways to help your child use the Internet safely and effectively:

- Spend time online together. Ask your child to show you some favorite websites. Talk about what she likes about each. If you don't have a computer, check your local library. Many have computers you can use.
- Help your child locate Internet sites that are appropriate for children her age. Talk about what the kinds of things you don't want in your home—games that are violent or include sexual content, for instance. You can install a "filter" on your computer. Check your Internet service provider to see what's available.
- Limit time online just as you limit TV time. Time spent sitting in front of any screen is time not spent outside playing or reading or just thinking.
- Make sure your child is safe. Tell your child never to tell anyone her real name or address. She must never arrange to meet anyone she has "talked" with in an online chat room. If anyone sends her messages that make her uncomfortable, she should tell you right away.

Developing Responsibility

Children who take responsibility and can work independently will do better in school. Here are some ways you can help your child:

Establish family rules. Children need and depend on rules. Have your child help you set the rules, then make sure you enforce them.

Post chores. Many families post a chart that outlines chores that need to be accomplished. Some families take turns, while others give certain jobs to certain people. Show your child how to break a job down into small steps, then to do the job one step at a time. This works for everything—getting dressed, cleaning a room, or doing a big homework assignment.

Let your child take responsibility. It's nine o'clock and your child announces he has a social studies project due tomorrow. Do you rush in to rescue him—perhaps staying up past midnight to type his report? Or do you let him suffer the consequences of putting it off?

The toughest lesson parents can sometimes teach children is to take responsibility for what they do, both at home and at school. Think of it this way—are you planning to type your child's papers at midnight when he's in college?

5
Early Adolescence

The early teen years (ages 12 to 14) are a time of rapid change. During these years, your adolescent will be learning to take responsibility for her own life. Just as in the earlier period of establishing a separate identity—the toddler years—your teen's striving for independence will sometimes create anxiety and distress for you.

This is also a time of enormous and rapid physical changes for young adolescents. Puberty usually begins between the ages of 10 and 14. What makes the teen years so difficult is that the change may begin any time during those years. So while teens may be the same *chronological* age, they will look and act very different from one another.

Teens regularly challenge authority. They are beginning to establish a code of behavior that is right for them. But experts say that teens are nearly as bewildered about the changes they're going through as you are.

Parenting is even more important at this age. By staying in touch and keeping your sense of humor, you can emerge from the teenage years with a relationship that will last a lifetime.

Parenting a Teenager

There's nothing easy about being the parent of a teenager, but here are some things that might help:

- Learn about adolescent development. Many of the things that worry you might actually be quite normal. Sooner or later, most teens have trouble. (When you feel that your teen's body has been taken over by an alien life form, it helps to know others are facing the same situation.)
- Remember your teenage years. Get out your high school yearbook and look again at the clothes you wore. This should help you keep things in perspective.
- Listen more than talk. Teens want and need parents who talk with them—but they need parents who listen even more. You might find that trips in the car or late-night chats are the best time to get your teen to open up.
- Teach your teen that rights and responsibilities go hand in hand. If she wants more rights, she must assume more responsibilities. Give your teen opportunities to take more responsibility in your family. Allow her to make more decisions for herself, and then face the consequences of those decisions.
- Use positive reinforcement whenever you can. The simple truth is that teens can tune out nagging and criticism.
- Spend quality time with your teen. He may tell you he doesn't want you to come to his baseball game. Go anyway. If he's watching TV, join him and then talk about what you saw.
- Help foster independence. Teens need to learn how to live on their own. A person who is responsible for washing some of the family's laundry, for example, is old enough to decide what to wear to school.

- Help your child become involved in the community. Teens need to find their place in the world. Whether it's by volunteering in a soup kitchen or taking part in a political campaign, community activism can help teens develop the self-confidence and skills they'll need in the future.
- Encourage other adults to spend time with your teen. Caring aunts and uncles, neighbors, or teachers can give your child support, guidance, and attention.
- You have feelings, too. Be sure you leave time to do some things for yourself, such as exercising, meditating, or spending time with friends. Get help if you feel overwhelmed.

Helping with Homework in the Early Teen Years

When your child's homework was learning 2 + 2 = 4, you probably felt pretty confident that you could help. But what happens when you can't remember how to solve for *x*? Do you have to stop helping your child with homework? Not at all. Even if you can't do the homework yourself, you can still provide help and support for your middle schooler.

Get organized. It's safe to say that most young teens have almost no ability to manage their time. Their thought process goes something like this: "My paper isn't due for a month? Hey, no problem—I'll watch TV today instead." You can help by making sure your teen gets organized. Many schools have homework planners—notebooks in which students write down all assignments and keep all their assignment sheets. If your teen's school doesn't use a planner, get one yourself.

Develop the homework habit. This is the age when assignments get longer. Teachers have higher expectations. And they *do* give homework. Set up a regular homework time at your house. During that time, you can work on paying bills or other paperwork. Your teen can work on homework—or spend the time reviewing and working ahead. Once this becomes a built-in habit, you might find that your teen *does* have math homework after all.

6

The High School Years

In general, older adolescents are searching for their own identity. Psychologist Dr. Haim Ginott says, "A teenager's task is tremendous, and the time is short." Through school activities, work, and friendships, teens are trying to discover who they are—and who they are not.

During the last years of adolescence, teens have four important responsibilities. They need to:

- Establish independence from both their family and their peers so they can move out into the world on their own.
- Develop relationships with members of the opposite sex.
- Prepare themselves for an occupation.
- Establish a meaningful system of values.

Establishing Independence

At this time, teens are striving to establish their near-total independence. This is an important step in helping them prepare for the time when they leave home. Whenever possible, you can help your older teen develop the skills she will need to succeed in the world by letting her know you have confidence in her ability to make choices. Use phrases like:

- "Consider the alternatives, but you decide."
- "The choice is up to you."
- "Here are my thoughts, but it's *your* decision."

Active listening is critical to keeping the lines of communication open during this period. Now is the time to begin treating your teenager the way you treat other adults. Be attentive to what your teen is saying. Stop what you're doing to focus on what your child has to say. Sometimes body language speaks much louder than words, so try looking for nonverbal cues to what's on her mind. Listen as much as you talk—and when you're talking, be sure to stop before your teenager stops listening.

Preparing for an Occupation

Teens want—and need—chances to develop a sense of responsibility. Many parents encourage their teens to find part-time jobs as a way of preparing them for the "real world." Sometimes they're successful. But when students work too much, their school work often suffers. The *Harvard Education Letter* cites several research studies showing that teens who work more than 15 hours a week:

- Get poorer grades
- Are more likely to use drugs and alcohol

- Are more likely to suffer from depression or anxiety
- Are less likely to go to college (Kelly, 1998)

Part-time jobs can teach teens important lessons, and given the cost of college tuition they might be an economic necessity for many families. But it's your job as a parent to make sure your teen keeps things in perspective. School is your teen's most important job. Any job has to come second.

Volunteer work is another way for teens to build their skills. Helping at a senior citizens' home, teaching a younger child to read, or working at a homeless shelter are ways teens can learn about their strengths and weaknesses as they help others in their community.

After-school activities can also help teens learn about careers. Self-discipline, leadership, and teamwork are just some of the things teens learn on the athletic fields and in the music room, while rehearsing for a play, or publishing the school newspaper.

All these are ways to show teens the options they have for their future, and especially the career they might choose. School counselors, of course, are there to help your teenager select the right high school courses and after-high-school training she will need to make her career choice a reality.

Establishing Values

The old adage that actions speak louder than words is never more true than when helping your adolescent establish his own system of values. It's hard for your teenager to accept the value of good citizenship if you never vote in an election. It's hard to see the importance of honesty if you boast about cheating on your income tax.

Communication is a crucial element in helping teenagers develop values. If you have a habit you're trying to change—starting an exercise program, for example—talk openly with your teen about what you're trying to do and why you're making the change. And don't be afraid to set firm limits and explain the reasons behind the rules.

Keeping the lines of communication open during your teenager's high school years will require extra effort on your part. Plan new activities to learn together. Perhaps you can both learn a new sport or sign up for a class together. (Nothing boosts a teenager's self-confidence so much as finding out he's better at something than Mom or Dad.) Find a project you can work on together to improve your home—perhaps you can paint a room or build a bookshelf. Also, many community agencies need volunteers. By working together on a project to improve your community, you will *both* feel better about your relationship—and about yourselves.

Developing Relationships with the Opposite Sex

Learning how to establish healthy relationships with members of the opposite sex is a crucial task of adolescence. By the time they're in high school, about half of all teens are sexually active. Nearly 1 million teenage girls each year become pregnant (Annie E. Casey Foundation, 1999). Most of these teens are unmarried, and most are not ready for the responsibilities and demands of parenthood.

Parents have an important role to play in helping teens delay sexual activity and thereby avoid the risk of teen pregnancy or parenting. Luckily, research shows that teens *want* their parents to talk with them about this sensitive issue. In fact, teens say parents are their *preferred* source of information about sex and health (Casey, 1999).

What can you do? Talk openly with your teen. Only you can teach your teenager your family and religious values on such issues as sexuality, pregnancy, contraception, and abortion. And only you can respond to your teen's specific situation, making sure she understands the consequences—and the risks—of early sexual activity. When communication between you and your teen becomes difficult, however, it's helpful to set up as many other support systems as you can for your teen. Friends, relatives, coaches, teachers, religious institutions—all of these can provide opportunities for adolescents to feel more secure and self-confident.

Peer Pressure

Teens take their first steps toward independence by establishing close relations with their peer group. Peers help teens learn about friendship, trust, and the importance of give-and-take in a relationship. With peers, teenagers learn social skills that will help them throughout their adult lives. But peers can also exert negative pressure. Teens often say they begin to use alcohol and drugs because "everybody's doing it." You'll need to:

Recognize that self-confidence is crucial to dealing with peer pressure. Teens who feel good about themselves are less likely to give in to pressure to try something they believe is wrong.

Anticipate situations and learn to deal with them. Help your teen develop some responses to dealing with pressure-filled situations.

Spend time listening to your teenager. Listening shows your teen you respect and value his opinions.

Help turn peer pressure into positive pressure. Teens themselves can be effective advocates of responsible behavior in areas such as drug and alcohol abuse. Programs like Students Against Drunk Driving (SADD) give teens the support they need to be reinforce positive behavior.

Know when to take the decision out of your teen's hands. Adolescents often *want* their parents' help in making tough decisions. It's easier for your teen to save face by saying "My parents won't let me go to parties where no adult is present" than to say "I feel uncomfortable at a party where there are drugs."

How Can I Tell if My Child Is Abusing Drugs or Alcohol?

Today, drugs and alcohol are so readily available that you can't assume that they will never affect your child. The National Institute on Drug Abuse (NIDA) found that by their senior year in high school, 78 percent of high school seniors and 47 percent of eighth graders have drunk alcohol. Nearly half (47 percent) of all high school seniors have used marijuana, and nearly 8 percent have used cocaine (NIDA, 2002). Here are some behaviors that may warn you:

- Abrupt change in mood or attitude.
- Sudden decline in attendance or performance at work or school.
- Impaired relationship with family or friends.
- Ignoring curfew.
- Borrowing an increased amount of money from parents or friends; stealing from family or employer.
- Heightened secrecy about actions and possessions.
- Associating with a new group of friends, especially those who use drugs (National PTA, 2002).

None of these indicators is proof that your teenager is experimenting with drugs; they may also indicate normal adolescent rebellion. But if you notice several of these changes in behavior—or if they continue and increase over time—you might want to take action to determine whether or not your child is involved with drugs or alcohol.

Where to Get Help

Raising children is like taking an 18-year course in child development. You always need to learn something new. Just as you think you have one stage of development mastered, your child changes and there's a lot more to learn.

A number of sources provide information on parenting. The resources listed at the back of this book offer suggestions on a number of resources for parents. If you have questions or concerns about parenting, you might contact:

Your child's school. Many schools offer evening courses on parenting. Some schools also sponsor support groups for students on such issues as drug use and coping with divorce.

Religious institutions. Many churches, temples, and mosques sponsor courses in parenting and counseling to families, and provide space for child care for working parents.

Mental health centers. Most offer free or low-cost counseling.

Your public library. Check for a listing of specialized resources in your community.

A Lifetime Commitment

"Children," says Neil Postman, "are living messages we send to a time we will never see." No legacy you will leave the world is more important than your children.

Being a good parent requires a tremendous investment—of time, energy, and unconditional love. And being a parent is a responsibility that continues throughout your child's life. The caring and support you show to your child as an infant and a toddler, from elementary school through high school, is just as important and appreciated as your child goes on to college and work. But the reward—watching your child grow into a responsible, caring adult—is truly priceless.

References

American Academy of Pediatrics. (2003). "Age-Related Safety Sheets." http://www.aap.org/family/1to2yrs.htm.

Ames, L. B., and Ilg, F. (1995). *Your one-year-old: The fun-loving, fussy 12- to 24-month old.* New York: Doubleday.

Ames, L. B., and Ilg, F. (1995). *Your two-year-old: Terrible or tender.* New York: Doubleday.

Ames, L. B., and Ilg, F. (1995). *Your three-year-old: Friend or enemy.* New York: Doubleday.

Ames, L. B., and Ilg, F. (1995). *Your four-year-old: Wild and wonderful.* New York: Doubleday.

Ames, L. B., and Ilg, F. (1995). *Your five-year-old: Sunny and serene.* New York: Doubleday.

Ames, L. B., and Ilg, F. (1995). *Your six-year-old: Loving and defiant.* New York: Doubleday.

Ames, L. B., and Ilg, F. (1995). *Your seven-year-old: Life in a minor key.* New York: Doubleday.

Ames, L. B., and Ilg, F. (1995). *Your eight-year-old: Lively and outgoing.* New York: Doubleday.

Ames, L. B., and Ilg, F. (1995). *Your nine-year-old: Thoughtful and mysterious.* New York: Doubleday.

Ames, L. B., and Ilg, F. (1995). *Your ten- to fourteen-year-old.* New York: Doubleday.

Annie E. Casey Foundation. (1999). *When teens have sex.* Baltimore: Annie E. Casey Foundation.

Bettleheim, B. (1987). *A good enough parent: A book on child-rearing.* New York: Vintage Books.

Brazelton, T. B. (1992). Touchpoints: *Your child's emotional and behavioral development.* Reading, MA: Addison-Wesley.

Children's Defense Fund. (2001). "25 key facts about America's children." http://www.childrensdefense.org/keyfacts.htm.

Christophersen, E. R. (1997). *Little people: Guidelines for common sense child rearing.* Shawnee Mission: Overland Press.

Coles, R. (1997). *The moral intelligence of children: How to raise a moral child.* New York: A Plume Book.

Cotton, K., and Wikelund, K. R. (2001). "*Parent involvement in education.*" NW Regional Educational Laboratory. http://www.nwrel.org/ scpd/sirs/3/cu6.html.

Henderson, A. T., and Berla, N. (1994). *A new generation of evidence: The family is critical to student achievement.* Washington, DC: National Committee for Citizens in Education.

Kelly, K. (1998). "Working teenagers: Do after-school jobs hurt?" *Harvard Education Letter,* July/August. http://www.edletter.org/past/issues/1998-ja/working.shtml/.

Kelly, M., and Parsons, E. (1992). *The mother's almanac* (rev.). New York: Doubleday.

Mayes, L. C., and Cohen, D. J. (2002). *The Yale child study center guide to understanding your child.* Boston: Little, Brown and Company.

National Association for the Education of Young Children. (1996). "10 signs of a great preschool." Washington, DC: NAEYC.

National Education Association. (2002). "A parent's guide to testing at your child's school" Washington, DC: NEA. http://www.nea.org/parents/testingguide.html.

National Institute on Drug Abuse. (2002). "InfoFacts: High school and youth trends." http://www.nida.nih.gov/Infofax/HSYouthtrends.html.

National PTA. (2002). "Common sense: Strategies for raising drug- and alcohol-free children." http://www.pta.org/commonsense/2parents/222signs.html.

Straus, M., Sugarman, D., and Giles-Sims, J. (1997). "Spanking by parents and subsequent antisocial behavior of children." *Archives of Pediatric and Adolescent Medicine,* 151: 761–767. http://www.unh.edu/frl/cp24art.htm.

U.S. Department of Education. (1993). *Helping your preschool child.* Washington, DC.

U.S. Department of Education. (2000). *Helping your child become a reader.* Washington, DC.

About the Author

Kristen Amundson has written educational materials for parents, school administrators, school board members, and students for more than twenty years. A former teacher and school board member, she has written extensively about parental involvement in education, reading, school violence, and preparing students for the 21st-century workplace.